Great Twentieth-Century Violin Concertos

IN FULL SCORE

Jean Sibelius

Edward Elgar

Alexander Glazunov

DOVER PUBLICATIONS, INC.

New York

Copyright

Copyright © 1995 by Dover Publications, Inc.
All rights reserved under Pan American and International Copyright Conventions.

Bibliographical Note

This Dover edition, first published in 1995, is a new compilation of three scores originally published separately. *Concerto / D minor / Violin and Orchestra / Jean Sibelius, Op. 47,* was originally published in an authoritative early edition [Schlesinger (Robert Lienau)], n.d. *Concerto pour Violon / avec Accompagnement d'Orchestre / composée par Alexandre Glazounow / Op. 82,* was originally published by M. P. Belaieff, Leipzig, 1905. *Concerto for Violin and Orchestra / by Edward Elgar / Op. 61,* was originally published by Novello and Company Limited, London, 1910. The Dover edition adds lists of contents and instrumentation and a glossary of German terms used chiefly in the Sibelius score.

Library of Congress Cataloging-in-Publication Data

Great twentieth-century violin concertos / Sibelius, Elgar, Glazunov. — in full score.
    1 score.
    Reprint (Sibelius). Originally published: Berlin : Schlesinger (Robert Lienau), [1905?].
    Reprint Glazunov. Originally published: Leipzig : M.P. Belaieff, 1905.
    Reprint (Elgar). Originally published: London : Novello, 1910.
    Contents: D minor for violin and orchestra, op. 47 (1903, revised 1905) / Jean Sibelius — A minor for violin with orchestral accompaniment (in one movement), op. 82 (1905) / Alexander Glazunov — B minor for violin and orchestra, op 61 (1909–10) / Edward Elgar.
    ISBN 0-486-28570-7 (pbk.)
    1. Concertos (Violin) — 20th century — Scores. I. Sibelius, Jean, 1865–1957. Concerto, violin, orchestra, op. 47, D minor. II. Glazunov, Aleksandr Konstantinovich, 1865–1936. Concertos, violin, orchestra, op. 82, A minor. III. Elgar, Edward, 1857–1934. Concertos, violin, orchestra, op. 61, B minor. IV. Title: Great 20th-century violin concertos.
M1012.G83 1995   95-751026
                                                       CIP
                                                       M

Manufactured in the United States of America
Dover Publications, Inc., 31 East 2nd Street, Mineola, N.Y. 11501

Contents

Glossary of German Terms

alle Bässe geteilt, all basses, divisi

B, B-flat
B nach A, change B-flat to A [timpani]
B nach H, change B-flat to B-natural [timpani]

D nach Des, change D to D-flat [timpani]
die Hälfte, half [of a string section]
die übrigen Bässe, the other basses
Dis, D-sharp

Es nach D, change E-flat to D [timpani]

Fis, F-sharp

Ges, G-flat
gest(opft), stopped [horn]
get(eilt), divisi
Gis nach A, change G-sharp to A [timpani]

H, B-natural
(1te, 2te) Hälfte, (1st, 2nd) half [of a string section]
His, B-sharp
H nach B, change B to B-flat [timpani]

nach, [change the pitch] to
natürlich, natural, usual [playing method]

offen, open [horn]

zu 2, a2

Dedicated to Franz von Vecsey

JEAN SIBELIUS

Concerto in D Minor
for Violin and Orchestra

Op. 47 (1903, revised 1905)

Instrumentation

2 Flutes [Flöte, Fl.]
2 Oboes [Hoboe, Hob.]
2 Clarinets in B♭ [Clarinette, Clar. (B)]
2 Bassoons [Fagott, Fag.]

4 Horns in F [Horn, Hrn.]
2 Trumpets in F [Trompete, Trp.]
3 Trombones [Posaune, Pos.]

Timpani [Pauken, Pk.]

Violin Solo [Violine Solo, Vl. S.]

Violins I, II [Violinen, Viol., Vl.]
Violas [Bratschen, Br.]
Cellos [Violoncelle, Vc.]
Basses [Bässe, Bass, B.]

I.

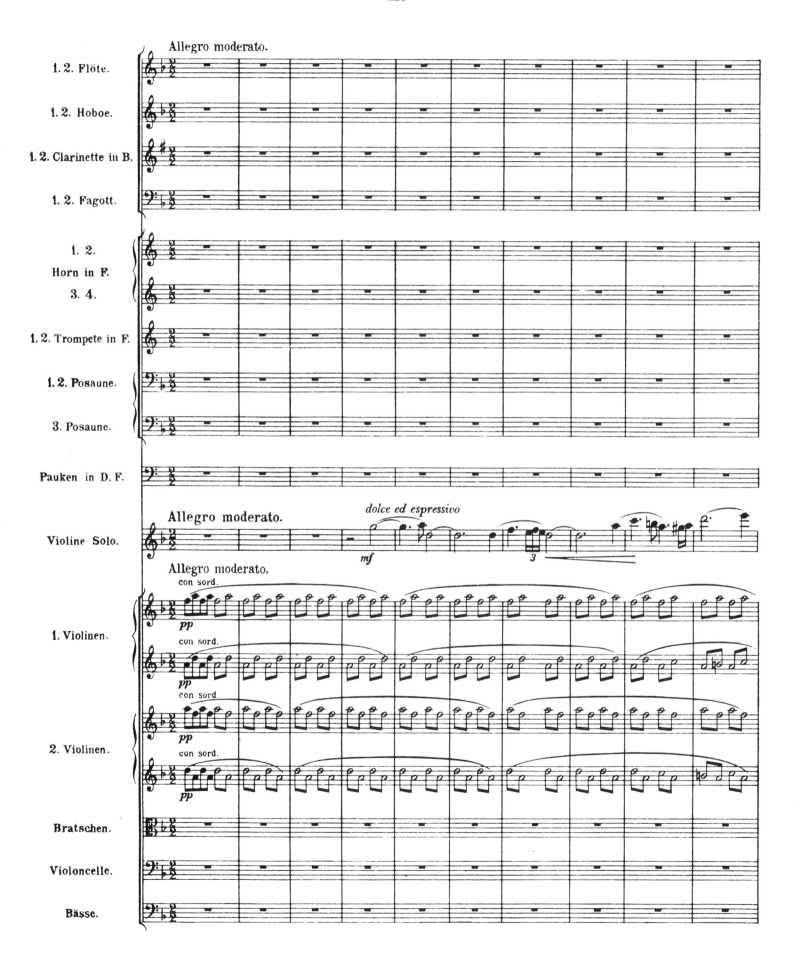

II.

III.

43

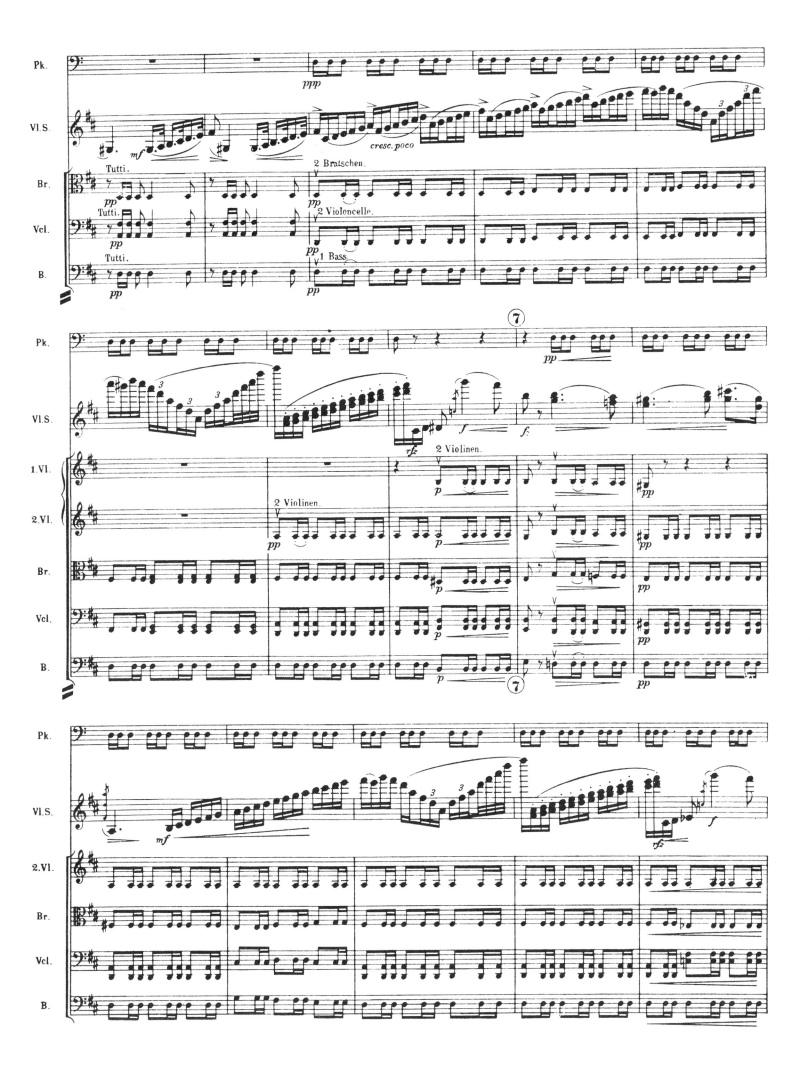

66 Sibelius, *Violin Concerto* (III)

ALEXANDER GLAZUNOV

Concerto in A Minor
for Violin with Orchestral Accompaniment

[in one movement]

Op. 82 (1905)

Instrumentation

Piccolo [Flauto piccolo, Fl. picc.]

2 Flutes [Flauti grandi, Fl. gr.]

2 Oboes [Oboi, Ob.]

2 Clarinets in A, B♭ [Clarinetti, Clar. (A, B)]

2 Bassoons [Fagotti, Fag.]

4 Horns in F [Corni, Cor.]

2 Trumpets in A, B♭ [Trombe, Tr-be. (A, B)]

3 Trombones ("poi")* [Tromboni, Tr-bni.]

Timpani [Timpani, Timp.]

Percussion:
    Cymbals [Piatti]
    Orchestra Bells ("poi")* [Campanelli, Camp.]
    Triangle [Triang(olo)]

Harp ("poi")* [Arpa]

Violin Solo [Viol(ino) Solo]

Violins I, II [Violini, Viol.]

Violas [Viole]

Cellos [Violoncelli, Vcelli]

Basses [Contrabassi, C. B.]

poi = "enters later"

84   Glazunov, *Violin Concerto*

To Fritz Kreisler

<small>EDWARD ELGAR</small>

Concerto in B Minor
for Violin and Orchestra

Op. 61 (1909–10)

"Aquí está encerrada el alma de…"*

*Elgar's inscription for the original edition: "Herein is confined the soul of…"

Instrumentation

2 Flutes [Flauti, Fl.]
2 Oboes [Oboi, Ob.]
2 Clarinets in A, B♭ [Clarinetti, Cl.]
2 Bassoons [Fagotti, Fag.]
Contrabassoon (*ad lib.*) [Contra Fagotto, C. Fag.]

4 Horns in F [Corni, Cor.]
2 Trumpets in A, B♭ [Trombe, Tr.]
3 Trombones [Tromboni, Trb.]
Tuba (*ad lib.*) [Tuba, Tb.]

Timpani [Timpani, Timp.]

Violin Solo [Vio(lino) Solo]

Violins I, II [Violini, Vio.]
Violas [Viole]
Cellos [Violoncelli, Vcl.]
Basses [Contra Bassi, C. B.]

I.

II.

III.

195

*) The **pizz.** tremolando should be "thrummed" with the soft part of three or four fingers across the strings.

END OF EDITION